William J. Standiford

FIRST-TIME HOMESELLER'S

ULTIMATE GUIDE

First-Time Seller's Ultimate Guide

Introduction to Selling Your Home

Welcome to the "First-Time Seller's Ultimate Guide." If you're reading this, you're likely about to embark on an exciting journey – the process of selling your home.

This guide is designed to provide you with the insights, knowledge, and tips you need to navigate this significant milestone with confidence.

Selling a home is more than just a transaction; it's a journey filled with emotions, memories, and possibilities. Your home has likely been a sanctuary, a place where you've laughed, celebrated, and made cherished memories. As you prepare to transition to a new chapter, it's important to recognize the emotional significance of letting go of a place that holds so much meaning.

Beyond the emotional aspects, selling a home also has financial implications that can shape your future. Your home is likely one of your most valuable assets, and the decisions you make throughout the selling process can have a significant impact on your financial well-being.

Whether you're downsizing, relocating, upgrading, or exploring new opportunities, we're here to guide you through every step of this journey. Selling a home can be complex, but with the right knowledge and guidance, it can also be a rewarding experience.

Throughout this guide, we'll explore the practical steps of selling your home, from preparing it for the market to navigating offers, negotiations, and the closing process.

We'll also delve into the emotional side of selling, offering insights to help you embrace this transition.

So, let's get started on this exciting path together. As you begin your journey as a first-time seller, remember that you're not alone – we're here to provide you with the information and support you need to achieve a successful sale and embark on your next adventure.

Welcome Message

Welcome to the First Time Home Seller's Ultimate Guide! Whether you're preparing to sell your home for the first time or looking for insights to enhance your selling experience, this guide is tailored to provide you with valuable information and expert guidance at every step.

As a dedicated real estate professional, I understand that selling your home is a pivotal decision. It's not just a transaction; it's a transition that holds emotional and financial significance. My aim with this guide is to empower you with the knowledge and confidence needed to navigate the selling process smoothly.

Within these pages, you'll find a wealth of advice, tips, and resources to help you make informed choices. From preparing your home and setting the right price to negotiating offers and finalizing the sale, we'll cover all aspects of the selling journey.

Journey of Selling Your Home: Selling a home involves multiple considerations, from understanding market conditions to effectively marketing your property. Here are a few reasons why selling your home can be both rewarding and strategic:

Unlocking Equity: When you sell your home, you can capitalize on the equity you've built over time. The proceeds from the sale can be used to invest in other opportunities or purchase your next dream home.

Embracing Change: Selling your home often signifies embracing a new chapter in your life. It's a chance to explore new locations, lifestyles, and possibilities that align with your evolving needs.

Maximizing Your Investment: Just as homeownership can be an investment, selling your home is an opportunity to maximize your returns. In a competitive market, well-priced homes can attract multiple offers, driving up the selling price.

Adapting to Market Trends: Understanding current market conditions and trends is crucial. It can help you strategize when to list your home, how to market it effectively, and how to position it competitively in the market.

Preparing for the Next Step: Selling your home opens the door to new opportunities. Whether you're downsizing, relocating, or upgrading, the sale provides the financial foundation for your next endeavor.

Contents:

About the Author & Reading this Book:

Hello, dear readers! I'm thrilled to have the opportunity to share a little glimpse into my world with you. My name is William Standiford, and I am a passionate writer and explorer of the boundless realms of imagination. I was born in Phoenix, Arizona and raised in Farmington, Missouri.

Throughout my life, I've worn many hats - from student to professional, traveler to dreamer - and each experience has shaped the stories I weave. I've wandered through the pages of history, dabbled in the realms of science fiction, and explored the intricate emotions of human relationships.

As it stands, I am an entrepreneur, business owner, and a Real Estate agent! In my free time I enjoy writing, singing, hiking, and building meaningful connections within the community. I enjoy listening to people's stories…it's interesting to see where people have been, what they've endured, and how they've triumphed in their personal and professional lives!

As you embark on this exciting journey, remember that you're not alone. As your trusted real estate advisor, I am here to guide you every step of the way. Together, we will work towards finding the perfect home that suits your needs, lifestyle, and budget.

Let's dive into the world of homeownership and make your dream of owning a home a reality! Feel free to reach out to me with any questions or concerns. I am thrilled to be a part of this significant moment in your life.

Happy reading and best wishes on your
home buying journey!

Willy Standiford
Real Estate Agent
Keller Williams STL
Direct: (660) 234-4261
Office: (314) 677-6000

Understanding the Selling Process

Selling a home involves a series of carefully orchestrated steps that culminate in a successful sale. Understanding these steps is essential to navigate the process smoothly and achieve the best possible outcome. Let's take a closer look at the journey you'll embark on as you sell your home.

Step 1: Preparation
Before listing your home, it's crucial to prepare it for the market. This involves tasks such as decluttering, deep cleaning, and making necessary repairs. First impressions matter, so enhancing your home's curb appeal and staging its interior can greatly impact potential buyers' perception.

Step 2: Pricing Strategy
Determining the right asking price for your home is a critical decision. It requires a combination of market analysis, understanding of local trends, and consideration of your home's unique features. A competitive price can attract more buyers, while an unrealistic price might discourage interest.

Step 3: Marketing and Listing
Once your home is ready, it's time to market it effectively. High-quality photos, compelling descriptions, and eye-catching online listings are essential to grab buyers' attention. Your real estate agent will create a strategic marketing plan to showcase your home's strengths.

Step 4: Showings and Open Houses
Buyers will want to see your home in person, so be prepared for showings and open houses. It's important to maintain your home's cleanliness and appeal during this

phase. Your real estate agent will manage these events and provide feedback from potential buyers.

Step 5: Receiving Offers
When offers start coming in, you and your agent will review each one. Factors to consider include the offer price, contingencies, and proposed closing date. Your agent will negotiate on your behalf to secure the best terms and highest price.

Step 6: Negotiation and Counteroffers
Negotiation is a common part of the selling process. Your agent will guide you through this phase, helping you respond to offers, negotiate terms, and reach a mutually beneficial agreement.

Step 7: Inspections and Appraisals
After accepting an offer, the buyer might conduct inspections to assess the home's condition. If necessary, negotiations can continue based on the inspection results. An appraisal will also be conducted to ensure the home's value aligns with the loan amount.

Step 8: Closing and Finalizing the Sale
Once all contingencies are met and the buyer's financing is secured, you'll move forward to the closing process. During the closing, legal documents will be signed, and ownership will be transferred to the buyer. The sale proceeds will also be distributed.

Importance of Timing and Market Conditions

The timing of your home sale can greatly impact its success. Market conditions, such as inventory levels and interest rates, play a significant role. In a competitive market with low inventory, your home might attract more attention, potentially resulting in multiple offers.

Conversely, market conditions can shift, affecting buyer demand. It's important to work closely with your real estate agent to monitor market trends and make informed decisions about the best time to list your home.

Additionally, personal timing considerations are crucial. Whether you're relocating for work, upgrading, or downsizing, aligning your selling timeline with your future plans is essential for a smooth transition.

Understanding the selling process and considering market conditions are pivotal to achieving a successful home sale. Your real estate agent will be your trusted guide, helping you navigate each step and make informed choices that lead to a positive outcome.

Preparing Your Home for Sale

When it comes to selling your home, first impressions matter. A well-prepared and inviting home can make all the difference in attracting potential buyers and securing a favorable deal. In this section, we'll explore essential steps to get your home ready for the market.

Home Staging and Decluttering Tips

Staging is the art of presenting your home in its best possible light to appeal to a wide range of buyers. Here's how to master the art of staging:

Declutter and Depersonalize: Start by decluttering each room. Remove personal items and excess belongings, allowing potential buyers to envision themselves in the space.

Create a Neutral Canvas: Opt for neutral colors in decor and furnishings. This helps buyers focus on the home's features rather than personal style.

Maximize Space: Arrange furniture to create an open and spacious feel. Rearrange or remove furniture if needed to improve traffic flow.

Let in Natural Light: Open curtains and blinds to let in natural light. Well-lit spaces appear larger and more inviting.

Add Subtle Accents: Use tasteful decor like fresh flowers, strategically placed cushions, and stylish artwork to add warmth and character.

Necessary Repairs and Improvements

Addressing necessary repairs and making strategic improvements can enhance your home's appeal and value:

Fix Visible Issues: Repair any visible defects such as leaky faucets, broken windows, or damaged flooring. Buyers appreciate a well-maintained home.

Consider Cosmetic Upgrades: Simple upgrades like fresh paint, updated hardware, and modern fixtures can breathe new life into your home.

Kitchen and Bath Updates: Kitchens and bathrooms hold special importance. Consider minor

upgrades like new countertops or faucets to enhance their appeal.
Check Electrical and Plumbing: Ensure that electrical and plumbing systems are in good working condition. Address any issues promptly.

Enhancing Curb Appeal

The exterior of your home is the first thing buyers see, so curb appeal is crucial:

Landscaping: Maintain a well-manicured lawn, trimmed bushes, and weed-free flower beds. Add potted plants or flowers to the entryway for a welcoming touch.

Entryway: A fresh coat of paint on the front door, a new welcome mat, and well-placed outdoor lighting can make your entryway inviting.

Exterior Maintenance: Repair or replace any damaged siding, roofing, or gutters. A well-maintained exterior assures buyers that the home is cared for.

Outdoor Living Spaces: If you have a patio or deck, arrange outdoor furniture to showcase potential entertaining areas.

By staging your home, addressing repairs, and enhancing curb appeal, you'll create a memorable and positive impression for potential buyers. This careful preparation sets the stage for a successful and rewarding home selling experience.

Setting the Right Price

Setting the right price for your home is a crucial step that significantly impacts your selling journey. Price it too high, and you risk scaring away potential buyers; price it too low, and you might not get the value your home deserves. In this section, we'll delve into the art and science of pricing your home effectively.

Importance of Accurate Pricing

Accurate pricing is the cornerstone of a successful home sale. Pricing your home correctly from the start can attract serious buyers, reduce time on the market, and increase your chances of receiving competitive offers. Overpricing can lead to your property languishing on the market, which may necessitate multiple price reductions and potentially lower offers down the line.

Utilizing Comparable Sales (Comps)

Comparable sales, often referred to as "comps," play a pivotal role in determining your home's market value. Comps are recently sold properties in your neighborhood that are similar to your home in terms of size, condition, features, and location. By analyzing comps, you can gain valuable insights into current market trends and set a competitive asking price.

Steps to Utilize Comps:

Research Recent Sales: Your real estate agent will help you identify properties that have recently sold in your area. These sales should have occurred within the past few months to reflect current market conditions accurately.

Compare Key Features: Analyze the features of the comps, such as the number of bedrooms and bathrooms, square footage, lot size, and amenities. This will help you understand how your property stacks up against others.

Adjust for Differences: If there are differences between your home and the comps—such as a larger yard or an additional bedroom—adjustments should be made to account for these variations.

Analyze Market Trends: Consider broader market trends, such as whether home prices are rising or falling in your area. This can provide additional context for your pricing decision.

Balancing Emotional Attachment with Market Value

Sellers often have an emotional attachment to their homes, which can influence their perception of value. While it's natural to appreciate the memories and experiences associated with your property, it's essential to balance this emotional attachment with the realities of the market. Emotional value doesn't always translate directly into market value.

Your real estate agent can provide an objective perspective and guide you toward an accurate pricing strategy. Their knowledge of local market trends, recent sales, and buyer preferences will help you make an informed decision that aligns with your financial goals.

Setting the right price requires a blend of research, market knowledge, and a clear understanding of your home's unique attributes. By pricing your home accurately, you'll increase your chances of attracting the right buyers and achieving a successful sale that benefits both parties.

Marketing Your Home Effectively

When it comes to selling your home, effective marketing is essential to attract potential buyers and showcase the best features of your property. In this section, we'll explore strategies to create a compelling listing, leverage high-quality visuals, and utilize various online platforms to maximize your home's exposure.

Crafting a Compelling Listing Description
Your listing description serves as your home's introduction to prospective buyers. It's crucial to provide a clear and captivating overview of your property's key features and benefits. Highlight unique selling points, such as upgraded amenities, spacious rooms, and any recent renovations. Keep the description concise while emphasizing the lifestyle your home offers. Use descriptive language that helps potential buyers visualize themselves living in the space.

Showcasing with High-Quality Photography and Virtual Tours

Photographs are often the first impression buyers have of your home. Invest in professional photography to capture your property in the best light, both figuratively and literally. High-quality images can emphasize architectural details, spaciousness, and the overall ambiance of each room. Additionally, consider offering virtual tours or video walkthroughs, allowing potential buyers to explore your home from the comfort of their own devices. Virtual tours can provide a comprehensive view of the layout and flow of the property, enhancing buyer engagement.

Leveraging Online Platforms and Social Media

The digital age has transformed the way homes are marketed. Online platforms and social media are powerful tools to showcase your home to a broad audience. Utilize reputable real estate websites to list your property, complete with professional photographs and a well-crafted description. Social media platforms like Facebook, Instagram, and YouTube can further expand your reach. Share visually appealing posts about your home, emphasizing its unique features. Engage with potential buyers by responding to comments and inquiries promptly.

Consider creating a dedicated hashtag for your property, allowing interested parties to easily find information and updates. Utilize local community groups and forums to spread the word about your home's listing. Collaborate with your real estate agent to strategically promote your property across various online channels.

Effective marketing is a pivotal aspect of selling your home. Craft a compelling listing description that highlights your home's unique features, invest in high-quality photography and virtual tours to engage potential buyers, and harness the power of online platforms and social media to expand your home's reach. By employing these strategies, you'll increase the likelihood of attracting qualified buyers and achieving a successful sale.

Navigating Offers and Negotiations
Receiving purchase offers is a significant milestone in the home selling process. This is where your hard work in preparing your home and effectively marketing it pays off. In this section, we'll delve into the intricacies of handling offers, employing negotiation strategies, and effectively managing counteroffers and contingencies.

Understanding Purchase Offers
When a potential buyer is interested in your property, they will submit a purchase offer. This offer outlines the terms and conditions under which they are willing to buy your home. It includes the proposed purchase price, the intended closing date, and any contingencies they may have.

It's essential to carefully review each offer with your real estate agent. Consider not only the offered price but also the proposed terms and contingencies. Some common contingencies include financing, home inspection, and appraisal contingencies. Understanding these contingencies is crucial, as they outline conditions that must be met for the sale to proceed.

Negotiation Strategies for the Best Deal
Negotiating with buyers requires a delicate balance of achieving the best possible outcome while maintaining a positive and respectful interaction. Your real estate agent will be your trusted advisor during this phase, providing insights into current market conditions and local trends.

Negotiation strategies can vary based on factors such as the number of offers, the urgency of the sale, and the condition of the market. It's essential to remain open to reasonable offers and be prepared to counteroffer when necessary. Remember that successful negotiations are about finding a mutually beneficial solution that satisfies both parties' needs.

Handling Counteroffers and Contingencies
Once you receive an offer, you have the option to accept, reject, or counteroffer. Counteroffers are common and are a natural part of the negotiation process. If the offered price isn't quite where you want it to be, or if there are certain terms you'd like to modify, a counteroffer allows you to propose changes.

Contingencies are conditions that the buyer must meet for the sale to proceed. These could include inspections, appraisals, or securing financing. As a seller, you may also have contingencies, such as the buyer providing a satisfactory earnest money deposit.
Your real estate agent will play a crucial role in managing negotiations, counteroffers, and contingencies. Their experience and expertise will guide you through this phase, ensuring that your interests are protected while maintaining open lines of communication with the buyer.

Navigating offers and negotiations requires careful consideration and effective communication. Understand the components of purchase offers, employ negotiation strategies that align with market conditions, and work closely with your real estate agent to manage counteroffers and contingencies. By approaching this phase strategically, you'll increase the likelihood of securing a successful and mutually beneficial deal.

The Home Inspection Process

The home inspection process is a critical step in the home selling journey. It provides both buyers and sellers with a comprehensive understanding of the property's condition and identifies any potential issues that may need attention. In this section, we'll delve into the importance of home inspections, how to address potential issues proactively, and the options available when issues are identified.

Importance of Home Inspections

A home inspection is a thorough examination of a property's structural and mechanical components. It helps buyers make informed decisions by uncovering any hidden defects or issues that might not be visible during a casual walkthrough. For sellers, a home inspection can reveal areas that need attention before listing the property, allowing them to address these concerns proactively.

Buyers often include a home inspection contingency in their purchase offers. This contingency gives them the right to have a professional inspector assess the property within a specified timeframe. If significant issues are discovered during the inspection, buyers can negotiate repairs or request a reduction in the purchase price.

Addressing Potential Issues Proactively

As a seller, addressing potential issues before listing your home can offer several advantages. It can enhance your property's appeal to potential buyers, expedite the selling process, and reduce the likelihood of last-minute negotiations based on inspection findings.

Before listing your home, consider having a pre-listing inspection. This allows you to identify any problems that may arise during the buyer's inspection. By addressing these issues upfront, you can present your home in the best possible condition and provide potential buyers with a clear understanding of its current state.

Options When Issues Are Identified

In some cases, issues may be uncovered during the buyer's inspection. When this happens, there are several options to consider:

1. **Addressing Repairs:** If the inspection reveals minor issues, you might choose to address them before the closing. This can alleviate concerns and demonstrate your commitment to a smooth transaction.
2. **Providing Credits:** Instead of making repairs, you can offer the buyer a credit toward the cost of addressing the identified issues. This allows the buyer to choose their preferred contractors and solutions.
3. **Negotiating Price:** Depending on the severity of the issues, you and the buyer can negotiate a reduction in the purchase price to account for necessary repairs.
4. **Walking Away:** If the inspection uncovers significant issues and the buyer is not comfortable

proceeding, they may choose to walk away from the deal. This underscores the importance of addressing potential issues proactively.

The home inspection process plays a pivotal role in the real estate transaction. Buyers gain a clearer picture of a property's condition, and sellers have the opportunity to address issues before they become obstacles. By recognizing the importance of home inspections, proactively addressing potential issues, and considering various options when issues are identified, you can navigate this phase successfully and ensure a smoother transaction for all parties involved.

Finalizing the Sale and Closing

The finalizing of a real estate sale and the closing process is the culmination of all the hard work put into selling your home. This stage involves reviewing the closing process, preparing for closing costs, and completing the necessary paperwork to transfer ownership to the buyer. In this section, we'll delve into the key aspects of finalizing the sale and guide you through the closing process.

Reviewing the Closing Process

Closing, also known as settlement, is the point at which ownership of the property is officially transferred from the seller to the buyer. It's a formal process that involves various steps, including:

1. **Title Search and Insurance:** A title search is conducted to ensure that there are no outstanding liens, judgments, or ownership disputes on the property. Title insurance is typically obtained to protect both parties from any unforeseen issues.

2. **Preparing Closing Documents:** Both the buyer and seller will receive a closing disclosure detailing the final terms of the transaction, including the purchase price, closing costs, and any adjustments.
3. **Signing the Documents:** The seller and buyer will sign a series of legal documents, including the deed transferring ownership. Additionally, any mortgage-related paperwork will be signed by the buyer.
4. **Funding and Disbursement:** The buyer's lender will fund the loan, and the funds necessary to close the transaction will be disbursed to the appropriate parties, including the seller, real estate agents, and other third parties.

Preparing for Closing Costs

Closing costs are the various fees associated with finalizing the sale of a home. These costs can include attorney fees, title insurance, appraisal fees, and more. It's important for both buyers and sellers to be aware of these costs and to budget accordingly. As a seller, you'll typically be responsible for covering your share of the closing costs, which can vary based on the terms of the sale and local customs.

Completing Necessary Paperwork

The paperwork involved in the closing process is essential to ensure a legally binding transfer of ownership. As a seller, you'll need to provide documents such as:

1. **Deed:** This legal document transfers ownership of the property from you to the buyer.
2. **Bill of Sale:** This document itemizes any personal property included in the sale, such as appliances or fixtures.

3. **Affidavits:** Depending on local laws and regulations, you may need to provide affidavits certifying that the property is free of certain conditions or liabilities.
4. **Closing Statement:** This document outlines the final financial details of the transaction, including the purchase price, prorated expenses, and closing costs.

The process of finalizing the sale and closing can feel complex, but with the guidance of a real estate professional, you can navigate it successfully. By reviewing the closing process, understanding and preparing for closing costs, and ensuring all necessary paperwork is in order, you're on your way to completing the sale of your home.

Remember, a knowledgeable real estate agent can provide valuable assistance throughout this process, ensuring that all the details are handled correctly, and the closing is as smooth as possible. With careful attention to these final stages, you'll soon be able to celebrate the successful sale of your property.

Moving On and Settling In

Congratulations! You've successfully navigated the process of selling your home and are now ready to embark on a new chapter. As you transition to your next adventure, it's important to ensure a smooth moving process, update your addresses and services, and embrace the opportunities that lie ahead. In this section, we'll explore valuable tips for making your move as seamless as possible and settling into your new home.

Tips for a Smooth Moving Process

Moving can be both exciting and overwhelming. Here are some tips to help you achieve a smooth transition:

1. **Plan Ahead:** Create a moving timeline that includes tasks like packing, hiring movers, and notifying important parties about your move.
2. **Declutter:** Before packing, take the opportunity to declutter and downsize your belongings. Donate or sell items you no longer need or want.
3. **Pack Strategically:** Start packing early and label boxes with their contents and destination rooms. Keep essential items like toiletries and clothes handy for easy access.
4. **Hire Professional Movers:** If possible, hire professional movers who can handle the heavy lifting and transportation of your belongings.
5. **Notify Important Parties:** Inform utility companies, the post office, banks, and other service providers of your change of address.
6. **Set Up Utilities:** Ensure that utilities like electricity, water, and internet are set up in your new home before you arrive.

Updating Addresses and Services

With a change of residence comes the task of updating your address and transferring services. Here's a checklist to guide you:

1. **Post Office:** Visit your local post office or update your address online to ensure your mail is forwarded to your new home.
2. **Government Agencies:** Update your address with the Department of Motor Vehicles, voter registration, and any other relevant government agencies.
3. **Financial Institutions:** Notify your banks, credit card companies, and other financial institutions of your new address.
4. **Subscriptions and Memberships:** Update your address for magazine subscriptions, online shopping accounts, and any memberships you hold.
5. **Healthcare Providers:** Inform your doctors, dentists, and other healthcare providers of your new address.

Embracing Your New Chapter

Settling into your new home is an opportunity to embrace a fresh start. Here are some ways to make the most of this new chapter:

1. **Explore Your Neighborhood:** Get to know your new surroundings by exploring local shops, restaurants, parks, and attractions.

2. **Meet Your Neighbors:** Introduce yourself to your new neighbors and build a sense of community.
3. **Personalize Your Space:** Unpack and arrange your belongings in a way that makes your new home feel comfortable and personalized.
4. **Create New Routines:** Embrace new routines that fit your new lifestyle and surroundings.
5. **Celebrate Achievements:** Take a moment to celebrate your accomplishments and the exciting journey you've undertaken.

Selling your home and moving to a new one marks a significant milestone in your life. By following these tips for a smooth moving process, updating your addresses and services, and embracing your new chapter, you're setting the stage for a successful transition. Remember, the process may come with its challenges, but with careful planning and a positive mindset, you can make your move a positive and fulfilling experience. As you settle into your new home, embrace the possibilities and opportunities that await you.

Common Challenges and How to Overcome Them

While selling your home can be an exciting and rewarding process, it's not without its challenges. From unexpected obstacles to managing stress and emotions, navigating these difficulties is an integral part of the journey. In this section, we'll explore some of the common challenges that sellers may encounter and provide strategies to overcome them.

Dealing with Unexpected Obstacles

1. **Home Inspection Surprises:** During the home inspection, issues may arise that you were not aware

of. It's essential to address these concerns promptly. Work with your real estate agent to determine whether repairs should be made or if a credit can be offered to the buyer.

2. **Low Appraisal:** If the appraised value of your home comes in lower than the agreed-upon sale price, it could jeopardize the transaction. Your real estate agent can help you navigate this situation by presenting comparable sales to support the price or negotiating with the buyer.
3. **Buyer Financing Challenges:** If the buyer faces difficulties obtaining financing, it could delay or even cancel the sale. Staying in communication with the buyer's lender and being open to potential solutions can help keep the transaction on track.

Managing Stress and Emotions

1. **Emotional Attachment:** Selling a home can bring up sentimental feelings, especially if you have fond memories associated with the property. It's essential to acknowledge these emotions while also focusing on the future and the opportunities your move will bring.
2. **Market Fluctuations:** The real estate market can be unpredictable, and factors beyond your control can impact the outcome of your sale. It's crucial to maintain a realistic outlook and work closely with your real estate agent to navigate changing market conditions.
3. **Timeline Pressures:** If you're trying to sell quickly due to job changes or other life events, the pressure can be stressful. Collaborate with your agent to

develop a strategic pricing and marketing plan to attract buyers promptly.

Strategies for Overcoming Challenges

1. **Communication:** Stay in close communication with your real estate agent throughout the process. They are there to guide you, provide expert advice, and help you make informed decisions.
2. **Flexibility:** Be prepared to adapt and adjust your plans based on changing circumstances. A flexible approach can help you overcome unexpected challenges.
3. **Focus on the Bigger Picture:** While challenges may arise, keep in mind the bigger picture and your end goal. Remember why you decided to sell and the positive outcomes you're working towards.
4. **Seek Support:** Lean on your support network, whether it's family, friends, or your real estate agent. Sharing your concerns can help alleviate stress and provide perspective.
5. **Practice Self-Care:** Selling a home can be demanding, both emotionally and physically. Make sure to take breaks, engage in activities you enjoy, and practice self-care to reduce stress.

Navigating challenges while selling your home is a natural part of the process. By recognizing common obstacles, staying proactive, and utilizing the support of your real estate agent and loved ones, you can overcome difficulties and achieve a successful sale. Remember that challenges can also present opportunities for growth and learning. Embrace the journey with a positive mindset, and you'll be well-equipped to overcome any hurdles that come your way.

Working with a Realtor: Your Path to Success

Selling your home is a significant endeavor that involves various complexities, from pricing and marketing to negotiations and paperwork. In this section, we'll delve into the benefits of working with a realtor and how their expertise simplifies the selling process, enabling you to achieve your goals with confidence.

Benefits of Professional Guidance

1. **Market Expertise:** A seasoned realtor possesses a deep understanding of the local real estate market. They can analyze market trends, assess comparable sales, and provide valuable insights to help you price your home competitively.
2. **Strategic Pricing:** Realtors are skilled in pricing strategies. They'll help you avoid the pitfalls of overpricing (which can deter buyers) or underpricing (which may lead to financial loss). A well-priced home attracts the right buyers and maximizes your returns.
3. **Targeted Marketing:** Marketing your home involves more than creating a listing. Realtors leverage their network, online platforms, and marketing tools to reach a wider audience. Their expertise ensures your property receives maximum exposure, increasing the chances of a swift and profitable sale.
4. **Negotiation Mastery:** Negotiating with buyers can be a daunting task. Realtors are trained negotiators who can advocate for your interests, navigate offers and counteroffers, and ensure you achieve the best possible terms.

5. **Transaction Management:** The paperwork and legalities involved in selling a home can be overwhelming. Realtors are well-versed in contracts and disclosures, ensuring that every detail is handled accurately and professionally.

How a Realtor Simplifies the Process

1. **Expert Advice:** A realtor is your go-to source for advice at every stage of the process. They can address your questions, provide insights, and guide you through difficult decisions, making the journey smoother and less stressful.
2. **Time and Convenience:** Selling a home demands time and attention. Realtors take on the legwork, from coordinating showings and marketing to managing inquiries and negotiations. This frees up your time to focus on your daily life.
3. **Objective Perspective:** Selling your home can be emotionally charged. A realtor provides an objective perspective, helping you detach from the emotional aspect and make decisions grounded in sound judgment.
4. **Problem Solving:** Challenges can arise during the process. A skilled realtor is equipped to handle unexpected issues, find solutions, and keep the transaction on track.
5. **Network of Professionals:** Realtors have a vast network of professionals, from inspectors and appraisers to contractors and attorneys. They can connect you with trusted experts who can assist with various aspects of the sale.

Working with a realtor is an investment in peace of mind and success. Their market knowledge, negotiation skills, and experience ensure you navigate the complexities of selling with ease. By entrusting your home sale to a professional, you can enjoy the benefits of a streamlined process, expert guidance, and the confidence that comes from knowing you're making informed decisions. Whether you're a first-time seller or have sold before, a realtor's support is invaluable on your journey to a successful home sale.

Resources and Tools for First-Time Sellers

Selling your home for the first time can feel like a complex endeavor. To make the process smoother and more manageable, it's important to have the right resources and tools at your disposal. In this section, we'll explore the essential elements that can guide you through your journey as a first-time seller.

Checklist for Selling Your Home

A comprehensive checklist serves as your roadmap throughout the selling process. It helps you stay organized and ensures you don't miss any crucial steps. Here's a snapshot of what a seller's checklist might include:

1. **Preparation Phase:**
    - Declutter and depersonalize your home
    - Make necessary repairs and improvements
    - Stage your home to showcase its best features
    - Enhance curb appeal
2. **Pricing and Marketing:**
    - Collaborate with your realtor to set an appropriate listing price

- Create a compelling listing description and gather high-quality photos
  - Utilize online platforms and social media to market your home
3. **Showings and Offers:**
   - Make your home available for showings and open houses
   - Evaluate purchase offers and negotiate with potential buyers
   - Address contingencies and move toward a successful sale
4. **Inspections and Negotiations:**
   - Navigate the home inspection process
   - Respond to inspection findings and negotiate repairs if needed
   - Continue negotiations until all parties are in agreement
5. **Closing and Transition:**
   - Prepare for the closing process and gather necessary documents
   - Review and sign closing paperwork
   - Hand over keys and officially transfer ownership

<u>Additional Resources</u>

Loan Program Information:

USDA:https://www.rd.usda.gov/programs-services/single-family-housing-programs/single-family-housing-guaranteed-loan-program

FHA:
https://www.hud.gov/federal_housing_administration

VA: https://www.va.gov/housing-assistance/home-loans/

Section 203k:
https://www.hud.gov/program_offices/housing/sfh/203k/203k--df

Conventional Loan Information (Found at Your Local Bank/Credit Union):
https://www.consumerfinance.gov/owning-a-home/loan-options/conventional-loans/

Missouri Housing Resources:

https://www.mohousingresources.com/

https://www.ago.mo.gov/docs/default-source/publications/landlord-tenantlaw.pdf?sfvrsn=4%20

HUD/Subsidized Housing Resources:

https://resources.hud.gov/

https://www.lowincomehousing.us/

Housing Counseling:

Help for Homeowners:
https://www.hud.gov/homeownerhelp

Help for Homebuyers:
https://www.hud.gov/topics/buying_a_home

Rental Assistance:
https://www.hud.gov/topics/rental_assistance

Recommended Texts:

First-Time Home Buyer: The Complete Playbook to Avoiding Rookie Mistakes - Scott Trench & Mindy Jensen

Your First Home: The Proven Path to Homeownership - Gary Keller & Jay Papasan

A Buyer's Life: A Concise Guide to Retail Planning and Forecasting - Dana Connell

Frequently Asked Questions for Sellers

Selling your home involves many details and decisions. To help address common questions you might have, we've compiled this list of frequently asked questions along with concise answers.

1. When is the best time to sell my home? The best time to sell depends on market conditions and your personal circumstances. Spring and early summer are generally popular due to increased buyer activity, but consulting with a realtor can provide insights tailored to your local market.

2. How should I price my home? Collaborate with your realtor to determine a competitive listing price. They'll analyze recent comparable sales (comps) in your area to help you set a price that aligns with market trends and your home's features.

3. Do I need to make repairs before listing? Making necessary repairs and improvements can enhance your home's appeal to buyers. Consult with your realtor to identify high-priority repairs that could impact your home's value or saleability.

4. What is home staging, and is it necessary? Home staging involves arranging and decorating your home to make it more appealing to potential buyers. While not mandatory, staging can help buyers visualize the space and often leads to faster sales.

5. How do I handle multiple offers? Your realtor will help you assess each offer's terms, including price, contingencies, and closing timeline. They'll guide you through negotiations and help you choose the offer that aligns best with your goals.

6. What are closing costs, and who pays them? Closing costs include various fees associated with finalizing the sale. They can include title insurance, attorney fees, and more. Both buyers and sellers have their own set of closing costs, and your realtor can provide an estimate.

7. How long does the closing process take? The closing process typically takes around 30 to 45 days. However, it can vary based on factors like the buyer's financing, inspections, and negotiations.

8. Do I need a home inspection? While not required, a home inspection is highly recommended. It provides a comprehensive assessment of your home's condition, helping you identify any potential issues that may need addressing before listing.

9. How can I prepare for showings and open houses? Clean, declutter, and depersonalize your home to create a welcoming atmosphere. Your realtor will guide you on preparing your home for showings, making it more appealing to potential buyers.

10. Can I sell my home while still living in it? Yes, you can sell your home while living in it. Your realtor will work with you to coordinate showings and provide tips for maintaining a presentable home during the selling process.

11. What is the role of a realtor in the selling process? A realtor guides you through the entire selling process, from pricing and marketing to negotiations and closing. They offer expertise, market insights, and handle the complexities, ensuring a smooth transaction.

12. How can I maximize my home's curb appeal? Enhance your home's curb appeal by maintaining your landscaping, painting the exterior if needed, and ensuring the front entry is inviting. A well-kept exterior makes a positive first impression.

Remember, your realtor is your best resource for personalized answers to your specific questions. Don't hesitate to reach out to them for guidance and support as you navigate the process of selling your home.

Glossary of Real Estate Terminology

Actual Cash Value

An amount equal to the replacement value of damaged property minus depreciation.

Adjustable-Rate Mortgage (ARM)

Also known as a variable-rate loan, an ARM usually offers a lower initial rate than a fixed-rate loan. The interest rate can change at a specified time, known as an adjustment period, based on a published index that tracks changes in the current finance market. Indexes used for ARMs include the LIBOR index and the Treasury index. ARMs also have caps or a maximum and minimum that the interest rate can change at each adjustment period.

Adjustment Period

The time between interest rate adjustments for an ARM. There is usually an initial adjustment period, beginning from the start date of the loan and varying from 1 to 10 years. After the first adjustment period, adjustment periods are usually 12 months, which means that the interest rate can change every year.

Amortization

Paying off a loan over the period of time and at the interest rate specified in a loan document. The amortization of a loan includes the payment of interest and a part of the amount borrowed in each mortgage payment.

Amortization Schedule

Provided by mortgage lenders, the schedule shows how over the term of your mortgage the principal portion of the mortgage payment increases and the interest portion of the mortgage payment decreases.

Annual Percentage Rate (APR)

How much a loan costs annually. The APR includes the interest rate, points, broker fees and certain other credit charges a borrower is required to pay.

Application Fee

The fee that a mortgage lender charges to apply for a mortgage to cover processing costs.

Appraisal

A professional analysis used to estimate the value of the property. This includes examples of sales of similar properties.

Appraiser

A professional who conducts an analysis of the property, including examples of sales of similar properties in order to develop an estimate of the value of the property. The analysis is called an "appraisal."

Appreciation

An increase in the market value of a home due to changing market conditions and/or home improvements.

Arbitration

A process where disputes are settled by referring them to a fair and neutral third party (arbitrator). The disputing parties agree in advance to agree with the decision of the arbitrator. There is a hearing where both parties have an opportunity to be heard, after which the arbitrator makes a decision.

Asbestos

A toxic material that was once used in housing insulation and fireproofing. Because some forms of asbestos have been linked to certain lung diseases, it is no longer used in new homes. However, some older homes may still have asbestos in these materials.

Assets

Everything of value an individual owns.

Assumption

A homebuyer's agreement to take on the primary responsibility for paying an existing mortgage from a home seller.

Balloon Mortgage

A mortgage with monthly payments based on a 30-year amortization schedule, with the unpaid balance due in a lump sum payment at the end of a specific period of time (usually 5 or 7 years). The mortgage contains an option to "reset" the interest rate to the current market rate and to extend the due date if certain conditions are met.

Bankruptcy

Legally declared unable to pay your debts. Bankruptcy can severely impact your credit and your ability to borrow money.

Capacity

Your ability to make your mortgage payments on time. This depends on your income and income stability (job history and security), your assets and savings, and the amount of your income each month that is left over after you've paid for your housing costs, debts and other obligations.

Closing (Closing Date)

The completion of the real estate transaction between buyer and seller. The buyer signs the mortgage documents and the closing costs are paid. Also known as the settlement date.

Closing Agent

A person who coordinates closing-related activities, such as recording the closing documents and disbursing funds.

Closing Costs

The costs to complete the real estate transaction. These costs are in addition to the price of the home and are paid at closing. They include points, taxes, title insurance, financing costs, items that must be prepaid or escrowed and other costs. Ask your lender for a complete list of closing cost items.

Closing Disclosure

A form that provides the final details of the selected mortgage loan. It includes the loan terms, projected monthly payments, and lists all fees and other costs to get the mortgage (closing costs). The lender is required to give the borrower the Closing Disclosure at least three business days before closing on the mortgage loan.

Collateral

Property which is used as security for a debt. In the case of a mortgage, the collateral would be the house and property.

Commitment Letter

A letter from your lender stating the amount of the mortgage, the number of years to repay the mortgage (the term), the interest rate, the loan origination fee, the annual percentage rate and the monthly charges.

Concession

Something given up or agreed to in negotiating the sale of the house. For example, the sellers may agree to help pay for closing costs.

Condominium

A unit in a multi unit building. The owner of a condominium unit owns the unit itself and has the right, along with other owners, to use the common areas but does not own the common elements such as the exterior walls, floors and ceilings or the structural systems outside of the unit; these are owned by the condominium association. There are usually condominium association fees for building maintenance, property upkeep, taxes and insurance on the common areas and reserves for improvements.

Contingency

A plan for something that may occur but is not likely. For example, your offer may be contingent on the home passing a home inspection. If the home does not pass inspection, you're protected.

Counter-offer

An offer made in response to a previous offer. For example, after the buyer presents their first offer, the seller may make a counter-offer with a slightly higher sale price.

Credit

The ability of a person to borrow money, or buy goods by paying over time. Credit is extended based on a lender's good opinion of the person's financial situation and reliability.

Credit Bureau

A company that gathers information on consumers who use credit. These companies sell that information to credit lenders in the form of a credit report.

Credit History

A record of credit use consisted of a list of individual consumer debts and a record of whether or not these debts were paid back on time or "as agreed." Credit institutions have created a detailed document of your credit history called a credit report.

Credit Report

A document used by the credit industry to examine your use of credit. It provides information on money that you've borrowed from credit institutions and your payment history.

Credit Score

A computer-generated number that summarizes your credit profile and predicts the likelihood that you'll repay future debts.

Creditworthy

Your ability to qualify for credit and repay debts.

Debt

Money owed from one person or institution to another person or institution.

Debt-to-Income Ratio

The percentage of gross monthly income that goes toward paying for your monthly housing expense, alimony, child support, car payments and other installment debts, and payments on revolving or open-ended accounts such as credit cards.

Deed

The legal document transferring ownership or title to a property

Deed of Trust

A legal document in which the borrower transfers the title to a 3rd party (trustee) to hold as security for the lender. When the loan is paid in full the trustee transfers title back to the borrower. If the borrower defaults on the loan the trustee will sell the property and pay the lender the mortgage debt.

Deed-in-Lieu of Foreclosure

A deed-in-lieu of foreclosure is a cancellation of your mortgage if you voluntarily transfer title of your property to your mortgage company. Usually you must try to sell your home for its fair market value for at least 90 days before a mortgage company will consider this option. A deed-in-lieu of foreclosure may not be an option if there are other liens on the property, such as second mortgages, judgments from creditors, or tax liens.

Default

Failure to fulfill a legal obligation. A default includes failure to pay on a financial obligation, but may also be a failure to perform some action or service that is non-monetary. For example, when leasing a car, the lessee is usually required to properly maintain the car.

Depreciation

A decline in the value of a house due to changing market conditions or lack of upkeep on a home.

Down Payment

A portion of the price of a home, usually between 3-20%, not borrowed and paid up front.

Earnest Money Deposit

The deposit to show that you're committed to buying the home. The deposit will not be refunded to you after the seller accepts your offer, unless one of the sales contract contingencies is not fulfilled.

Equity

The value in your home above the total amount of the liens against your home. If you owe $100,000 on your house but it is worth $130,000, you have $30,000 of equity.

Escrow

The holding of money or documents by a neutral third party before closing. It can also be an account held by the lender (or servicer) into which a homeowner pays money for taxes and insurance.

Fixed-Rate Mortgage

A mortgage with an interest rate that does not change during the entire term of the loan.

Forbearance

Your lender may offer a temporary reduction or suspension of your mortgage payments while you get back on your feet. Forbearance is often combined with a reinstatement or a repayment plan to pay off the missed or reduced mortgage payments.

Foreclosure

A legal action that ends all ownership rights in a home when the homebuyer fails to make the mortgage payments or is otherwise in default under the terms of the mortgage.

Gift Letter

A letter written by a family member verifying that a certain amount of money was given to you as a gift and that you don't have to repay it. You can use this money toward a portion of your down payment with some mortgages.

Gross Monthly Income

The income you earn in a month before taxes and other deductions. It may also include rental income, self-employed income, income from alimony, child support, public assistance payments, and retirement benefits.

Home Inspection

A professional inspection of a home to determine the condition of the property. The inspection should include an evaluation of the plumbing, heating and cooling systems, roof, wiring, foundation and pest infestation.

Homeowner's Insurance

A policy that protects you and the lender from fire or flood, which damages the structure of the house; a liability, such as an injury to a visitor to your home; or damage to your personal property, such as your furniture, clothes or appliances.

Housing Expense Ratio

The percentage of your gross monthly income that goes toward paying for your housing expenses.

Index

The published index of interest rates used to calculate the interest rate for an ARM. The index is usually an average of the interest rates on a particular type of security such as the LIBOR.

Individual Retirement Account (IRA)

A tax-deferred plan that can help you build a retirement nest egg.

Inflation

An increase in prices.

Inquiry

A request for a copy of your credit report. An inquiry occurs every time you fill out a credit application and/or request more credit. Too many inquiries on a credit report can hurt your credit score.

Interest

The cost you pay to borrow money. It is the payment you make to a lender for the money it has loaned to you. Interest is usually expressed as a percentage of the amount borrowed.

Keogh Funds

A tax-deferred retirement-savings plan for small business owners or self-employed individuals who have earned income from their trade or business. Contributions to the Keogh plan are tax-deductible.

Liabilities

Your debts and other financial obligations.

Lien

A claim or charge on property for payment of a debt. With a mortgage, the lender has the right to take the title to your property if you don't make the mortgage payments.

Loan Estimate

A written statement from the lender itemizing the approximate costs and fees for the mortgage. A lender is required to provide potential borrowers with a loan estimate within three business days of receiving a loan application.

Loan Modification

This is a written agreement between you and your mortgage company that permanently changes one or more of the original terms of your note to make the payments more affordable.

Loan Origination Fees

Fees paid to your mortgage lender for processing the mortgage application. This fee is usually in the form of points. One point equals 1% of the mortgage amount.

Lock-In Rate

A written agreement guaranteeing a specific mortgage interest rate for a certain amount of time.

Low-Down-Payment Feature

A feature of some mortgages, usually fixed-rate mortgages, that helps you buy a home with as little as a 3% down payment.

Margin

A percentage added to the index for an ARM to establish the interest rate on each adjustment date.

Market Value

The current value of your home based on what the purchaser would pay. An appraisal is sometimes used to determine market value.

Mortgage

A loan using your home as collateral. In some states the term mortgage is also used to describe the document you sign [to grant the lender a lien on your home]. It may also be used to indicate the amount of money you borrow, with interest, to purchase your house. The amount of your mortgage is usually the purchase price of the home minus your down payment.

Mortgage Broker

An independent finance professional who specializes in bringing together borrowers and lenders to complete real estate mortgages.

Mortgage Insurance (MI)

See Private Mortgage Insurance.

Mortgage Lender

The lender provides funds for a mortgage. Lenders also manage the credit and financial information review, the property and the loan application process through closing.

Mortgage Rate

The cost or the interest rate you pay to borrow the money to buy your house.

Mutual Funds

A fund that pools the money of its investors to buy a variety of securities.

Net Monthly Income

Your take-home pay after taxes. It is the amount of money that you actually receive in your paycheck.

Offer

A formal bid from the homebuyer to the home seller to purchase a home.

Open House

When the seller's real estate agent opens the seller's house to the public. You don't need a real estate agent to attend an open house.

Points

1% of the amount of the mortgage loan. For example, if a loan is made for $50,000, one point equals $500.

Pre-Approval Letter

A letter from a mortgage lender indicating that you qualify for a mortgage of a specific amount. It also shows a home seller that you're a serious buyer.

Pre-Qualification Letter

A letter from a mortgage lender that states that you're pre-qualified to buy a home, but does not commit the lender to a particular mortgage amount.

Predatory Lending

Abusive lending practices that include making mortgage loans to people who do not have the income to repay them or repeatedly refinancing loans, charging high points and fees each time and "packing" credit insurance onto a loan.

Principal

The amount of money borrowed to buy your house or the amount of the loan that has not yet been repaid to the lender. This does not include the interest you will pay to borrow that money. The principal balance (sometimes called the outstanding or unpaid principal balance) is the amount owed on the loan minus the amount you've repaid.

Private Mortgage Insurance (PMI)

Insurance needed for mortgages with low down payments (usually less than 20% of the price of the home).

Property Appreciation

See Appreciation.

Rate Cap

The limit on the amount an interest rate on an ARM can increase or decrease during an adjustment period.

Ratified Sales Contract

A contract that shows both you and the seller of the house have agreed to your offer. This offer may include sales contingencies, such as obtaining a mortgage of a certain type and rate, getting an acceptable inspection, making repairs, and closing by a certain date.

Real Estate Professional

An individual who provides services in buying and selling homes. The real estate professional is paid a percentage of the home sale price by the seller. Unless you've specifically contracted with a buyer's agent, the real estate professional represents the interest of the seller. Real estate professionals may be able to refer you to local lenders or mortgage brokers, but are generally not involved in the lending process.

Refinance

Getting a new mortgage with all or some portion of the proceeds used to pay off the original mortgage.

Reinstatement

Your lender may agree to let you pay the total amount you are behind, in a lump sum payment and by a specific date. This is often combined with forbearance when you can show that funds from a bonus, tax refund, or other source will become available at a specific time in the future. Be aware that there may be late fees and other costs associated with a reinstatement plan.

Repayment Plan

This is an agreement that gives you a fixed amount of time to repay the amount you are behind by combining a portion of what is past due with your regular monthly payment. At the end of the repayment period you have gradually paid back the amount of your mortgage that was delinquent.

Replacement Cost

The cost to replace damaged personal property without a deduction for depreciation.

Short Payoff (Short-Sale)

If you can sell your house but the sale proceeds are less than the total amount you owe on your mortgage, your mortgage company may agree to a short payoff and write off the portion of your mortgage that exceeds the net proceeds from the sale.

Title

The right to, and the ownership of, property. A title or deed is sometimes used as proof of ownership of land.

Title Insurance

Insurance that protects lenders and homeowners against legal problems with the title.

Truth-In-Lending Act (TILA)

Federal law that requires disclosure of a truth-in-lending statement for consumer loans. The statement includes a summary of the total cost of credit, such as the APR and other specifics of the loan.

Underwriting

The process a lender uses to determine loan approval. It involves evaluating the property and the borrower's credit and ability to pay the mortgage.

Uniform Residential Loan Application

A standard mortgage application your lender will ask you to complete. The form requests your income, assets, liabilities, and a description of the property you plan to buy, among other things.

Warranties

Written guarantees of the quality of a product and the promise to repair or replace defective parts free of charge.

Conclusion

Congratulations on successfully navigating the journey of selling your home! As you complete this significant chapter, take a moment to celebrate your accomplishments and reflect on the valuable experience you've gained. This concluding section serves as a final guidepost, offering insights into celebrating your successful sale and embracing the lessons from your real estate journey.

Celebrating Your Successful Sale

Selling your home is no small feat—it's a culmination of careful planning, strategic decisions, and collaborative efforts. Now that you've reached the finish line, it's time to celebrate your achievement. Here are a few ways to honor this milestone:

1. **Host a Celebration:** Invite friends and family to a gathering to mark this achievement. Sharing your success with loved ones adds a meaningful touch to your journey.
2. **Capture Memories:** Take photos of your home before you move out. These snapshots will serve as cherished memories of the space where you've made countless moments.
3. **Celebrate Generosity:** Consider donating items you no longer need to local charities or shelters. It's a way to pay it forward and make a positive impact in your community.
4. **Document the Process:** Write down your thoughts and feelings throughout the selling process.

Reflecting on Your Real Estate Journey

Your journey as a home seller has imparted valuable lessons that extend beyond the transaction itself. Take a moment to reflect on the wisdom you've gained and the growth you've experienced:

1. **Knowledge is Power:** You've gained a deep understanding of the real estate market, pricing strategies, negotiation tactics, and more. This knowledge empowers you for future real estate endeavors.
2. **Embracing Change:** Selling a home requires adapting to change, making tough decisions, and embracing new opportunities. These skills will serve you well in various aspects of life.
3. **Collaboration and Communication:** Your interactions with real estate professionals, buyers, and service providers have enhanced your communication and collaboration skills.
4. **Financial Awareness:** The financial aspects of selling a home have provided insights into budgeting, understanding market values, and making informed choices.
5. **Confidence:** Successfully selling your home has likely boosted your self-confidence and shown you the rewards of careful planning and execution.

Your Journey Continues

As one chapter closes, another opens. Your real estate journey doesn't end with the sale of your home; it transitions into new possibilities and opportunities. Whether you're moving to a new space, investing in real estate, or simply exploring new horizons, the experiences you've gained as a home seller will continue to guide you.

Remember, you're never alone on this journey. Real estate professionals, friends, and family are here to support and advise you. As you embrace the lessons and memories from this process, you're equipped to approach future endeavors with wisdom and confidence.

Thank you for allowing me to be a part of your real estate journey. It's been a pleasure guiding you through the process and witnessing your success. If you have any further questions or if there's anything else I can assist you with, please don't hesitate to reach out.

Best wishes on your ongoing journey, and may your future endeavors be as rewarding as your successful home sale!

www.ingramcontent.com/pod-product-compliance
Lightning Source LLC
Chambersburg PA
CBHW071106260726
48661CB00006B/2490